i am not
a practicing
angel

I look good
together

Got these penny wings
I could actually fly with

It all becomes so clear

Sound goes down
Sanity returns in an instant
The night is bigger...

I'd rather stay near the ground
I'm not a practicing angel

from Puppet X
by Jerry Ratch

poems by alta

i am not
a practicing
angel

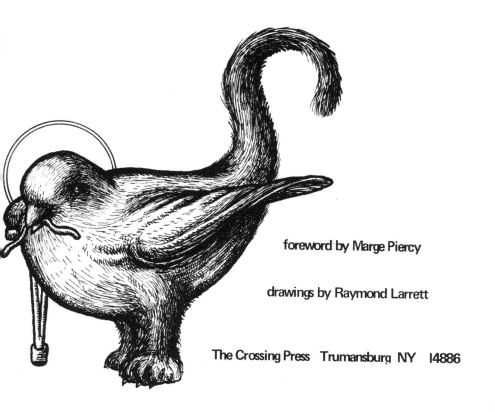

foreword by Marge Piercy

drawings by Raymond Larrett

The Crossing Press Trumansburg NY 14886

ACKNOWLEDGEMENTS

Never Mind, Orgasm, Age, Second Wave, Women—A Journal of Liberation, 1941, New, Mt. Moving Day, Everywoman, Aldebaran Review, Manroot, Shameless Hussy Review, Poetry Now, Woman's Press, Country Press, 4th World, Off Our Backs, Moving Out, Second Coming

Design by Charlotte Cohen

Library of Congress Cataloging in Publication Data

Alta.
   I am not a practicing angel.

   I.   Title
PS3551.L7612   811'.5'4   74-32443
ISBN 0-912278-54-4
ISBN 0-912278-55-2 pkb.

foreword

She doesn't say more—or less—than she means.
Her poems drop into your mind like stones
and set up vibrations. Not angelic or demonic,
not grand or overinflated, not studious or
posey, what she writes is as human and daily
and nourishing as good soup. She has a salty
sense of humor. Poems of the kitchen, the
bedroom, and the street, and of herself as
character caught and speaking.

—Marge Piercy

i want to say the words that take you back there.
wherever you'd like to be.
was there a lamp in the window?
a bowl of fruit you could really eat?
plants hanging from the ceiling in pots in the bathroom?
what was there you liked,
there, where
you'd like to be again.

for me it's steam on the windows,
snow delicately waiting on the dark twigs.
the moon between clouds &
the smell of someone i love.
crisp taco all drippy with oil.
love it love it love it love it

NEVADA

  & so i walk
like a cowboy.
tumbleweeds chase
my legs, tangle
my ankles. icy water
to step into. snow still
on the banks.
taste first the snow,
then water. pine
cones. needles dry on the ground. a cozy
gathering of pines &
water & feet without boots
daddy was the only one
who could stand in those
cold cold streams.
music is my heritage.

EURIDICE

all the male poets write of orpheus
as if they look back & expect
to find me walking patiently
behind them. they claim i fell into hell.
damn them, i say.
i stand in my own pain
& sing my own song.

why do you write they ask
why do you breathe i ask

POET

i remember the whisper from when i was a kid.
"you're different" & always i retorted
"everyone's the same!" angry everytime a hippie
said "plastic people" angry everytime a white
said "darkie" sick of all the names bourgeois,
& commie, chick & the voice insisting "look.
they know yr different" & it was right but for
years i shuffled, trying to go their direction
at their speed but they always knew i was more different
than i knew they were more alike.

i have to learn to write the
new mysteries just as i had
to learn to write the poems,
& again there is no teacher

it is a bright rain.
full moon behind the clouds
gives it a daylight aspect.
i fear irrational things;
men with teeth.

i am terrified (but that is nothing new)
    i wake, startled
    & touch his face with terrified fingers;
    has he really not changed form.

my hands make circles around the children;
my feet make circles on the floor.
once my arms formed a cross & aimed
themselves at the back door
(do not let writing this erase that protective power)

                the baby cries her dreams / i am terrified
                        in this bright rain.

EINSAME NACHT: Hesse

Die ihr meine Bruder seid
Arme Menschen nah und ferne
Die ihr im Bezirk der Sterne
Tröstung träumet eurem Leid,
Die ihr wortelos gefaltet
In die blass gestirnte Nacht
Schmale Dulderhände haltet,
Die ihr leidet, die ihr wacht,
Arme, irrende Gemeinde,
Schiffer ohne Stern und Glück —
Fremde, dennoch mir Vereinte,
Gebt mir meinen Gruss zurück!

TRANSLATION
LONELY NIGHT

sisters & brothers,
poor people, near & far
gazing lunatic at stars
dreaming of relief from yr sorrow,
you whom the words fail,
hold out small thin hands
in the starshocked night;
what do you hope, what do you watch
poor sailors
ship without star or luck —
you are my companions
return my greeting.

WIE SIND DIE TAGE: Hesse

Wie sind die Tage schwer!
An keinem Feuer kann ich erwarmen,
Keine Sonne lacht mir mehr,
Ist alles leer
Ist alles kalt und ohne Erbarmen
Und auch die lieben klaren
Sterne schauen mich trostlos an,
Seit ich im Herzen erfahren,
Das Liebe sterben kann.

TRANSLATION
HOW GO THE DAYS

how heavy the days are!
at no fire can i warm myself,
no sun laughs with me,
it's all empty,
all cold & without mercy,
& even the clear
stars shine on me without joy
since it has entered my heart
that love can die.

the brittle leaves
trembling on their stems

& maybe i'll just sit here writing poems
maybe i'll just sit here feeling good
& writing poems & wait for my eager
legs to walk me outside in the
morning, in the sun in the morning
in san francisco

barefoot lady bouncing on the grass,
yr shadow w/o end

SENSIBLE QUESTION

who the hell are you
to throw the first stone?

the day mrs. savage cut off my welfare we had a party.
they won this round, the tattletale neighbors, the conservative doctor,
all those who told savage i was living in sin with a man a man
living in sin with a man a man a man
so we gave that man breakfast in bed
(what's this for?) he said & we celebrated
& tore up paper for confetti & showered it on his surprised head
(o hey!) he said
& mrs. petress the lawyer said we would fight it &
the man said he would try to pay all the bills this month
& i couldnt buy the kids gum in the gum machine cause all the pennies
i had had to get us home on the bus & the driver was a human man & didnt
make the kids pay fare (only 15¢ for the little tykes)
so we came home & split the cold orange in the icebox after being so hot
on the long walk home & the baby just came in saying
"yr knee hurts so i giving you dis flower"
& we celebrate our love for one another & we
stand tall in our second hand clothes & up yr ass with a silver dollar,
savage welfare. we'll get what you owe us
we'll get it all!

yr hot buns on mine in the dark
& the whole world is our warm bed
there must be joy like this every
                              where forever
my toes tucked between yr legs
i want it to last
sing a little song in my head
to remember by
next time i'm cold at a bus stop
i'll sing warm buns in my bed
& my punkin Ado who loves me.

he has been shy
these 2 weeks. people asked him
not to music so loud
(the rite 1/2 of their brains
atrophied)
& last nite, our guests
left while he was playing.
he cuddles into my arm
under the sheets & i love him.
i would wish him
none of those insults.

the scent of the sea, & the
mist of it. his thin
white legs next to me: i kiss
the inside of his knee & his
toes wiggle happy.
birds wheeling round kites in the sky.

it is always a surprise
how gentle yr fingers.

(but when i asked
do you want to hear this poem,
you forgot, or didnt hear me.)

you turn over & cough.
i pray for a love that grows.

secretly i fear there is
something ridiculous about me.
why else would people laugh
when i speak?

fighting my dependency:
keeping busy, having lunch
with friends, printing my book.
when you're away i feel like
i'm only wearing one shoe.

like stone
we turn to stone
trapped in the joy
of timelessness

like stone our postures
caught in time
everyone will know
how we loved,
we loved

HIWAY 40

the trucks going forever down the hiway
between the movie show & the post office.
& people walking when the green light says WALK
                    reno
san lorenzo

        fresno
long beach

                    van horn

& the square grey trucks
& the flat western towns

in the Red Star Cafe she brags
'i can always tell a truck driver!'
he says 'hell you can.'
she says 'oh, yes.'
he says 'how?'
'by their beam!'
he leans forward, suggests, 'you tell me, then,
what do i do?'
she puts down the cups, walks out from the counter
wiping her hands on her apron, looks at his behind
& roars 'man, you are a *truck driver!*'

the full clouds heavy
on the low grey roofs

i wait in the standard station;
the pepsi machine hums,
the chair has old milkshake dribbled on it.
i am waiting for the bank to open so i can
cash my $4.50 check. i watch the trucks
lunge down the hiway.

nulaid foods.
navajo.
p.i.e. (wow! i havent seen a p.i.e. truck
since i was a little kid: hiway 40)

the sun warm thru the dusty window.

F-310 gas. free cups with a full tank.
trailers, busses, u-hauls, a slatted
pickup with brooms & shovels standing guard.

i met my love in a mobil station.
tryin to con him into lettin me use the phone for free.

a plumber's truck. a beige ford with its fender crushed.
the orange school bus with lil black stripes to remind you
what school *really* is.

volunteers of america.
(in costa rica they didnt like it when i called myself american.
that's what *they* are. they called me yankee. & one even told me to
go home!)

the official man came in wearing a white shirt
& a lil blue hat & he's takin the money out of the pepsi machine.
sounds like a goddamn slot machine: clang clang ka chonk ka chonk

& him pickin up dimes off the floor

what do the interminable trucks on these hiways
have to do with the women who live alone
in apartments with undistinguishable furniture?

(what do any of us have to do
with the rest of us?)

a roomful of guys just back from 'nam,
getting rehabilitated, learning to use plastic legs;
in 3 weeks they'll be able to walk all the way
to the corner to meet the pusher.
the other pusher, not the one who pushed them in front
of the bullets & flak, some other pusher who works
for some other pusher, who may know someone who knows the 1st
pusher, the one who makes money off that war.
they're probably different pushers, wouldnt you suppose?
probly not the same pusher is cruel enuf to cripple these
fine young men & get them hooked besides, must be 2 pushers.
2 guys up there, pulling strings to the goosestepping puppets
w/burned out eyes. probly not 1 pusher. probly 2 pushers.
or maybe its a whole corporation?

MONOGAMY AINT 1/2 BAD

for Angel

i love it when you shove it.

A PLAY

man & woman,
fully dressed,
rolling on floor.

feminist jumps between them
   "STOP! dont sell out yr sisters!"

husband jumps between them
   "STOP! arent i man enuf for you?"

kids jump between them
   "dont make another divorce!"

woman writhes
on floor; man
bends into himself,
his hand on his crotch.

they arduously move away from the others,
reaching out to each other
a priest jumps between
   "STOP! fantasize, like i do!
   that way you'll stay faithful!"

woman turns away, ARGHHH!

she & lover stand,
try to spot each other
over the others.
reach out &
touch

a telephone rings
a girl scout troop
begins nature study
at their feet.

TOO BAD I DONT CHARGE

my life revolves around my cunt
my cunt revolves around yr penis
hard up & blood red shooting
white sperm that dies inside me
so i won't die enjoying myself to
death & its hot all the time it
feels hotter than my pink thighs
it feels hotter than hungry fingers
hot as a gushing penis & neither
hot nor cold cools me down it'll
just have to wear out & my door
locked but then i'd climb out the
windows or let you in so what the
fuck, fuck me hotter deeper do it
do it! i tire of work & people &
enlightenment. i want sex.

HER STORY

the slaves were freed
to stand eating salt pork
to defend themselves, unarmed
against the armed kkk.
some whites expect blacks
to be grateful.

women were freed
to vote for nixon or mcgovern
to defend themselves, unarmed,
against armed rapists.
some men expect women
to be grateful.

ALCHEMY/
to turn lead into gold: to turn pain into poems

for Pat

1.

i havent written about this
because it's going to hurt.
it's going to hurt her & it's
going to hurt me.
she's never said
"stop being racist"
& i've never said
"do i act like i been raised
english?"
i call her when i'm in trouble,
but it was 2 years
before i went to see her in her home.

ll.

i'm so revolutionary
when i find out
my black lovers
have black wives,
i stop seeing them.

lll.

i'm no racist.
i've slept with black men.
no indians or chicanos
or chinese or japanese,
but shit i cant cover the whole world.
havent slept with any black women
but thats not my fault.
& i didnt stay away from pat's house
cause she was black,
i stayed away cause
i was afraid.
that neighborhood
was unfamiliar to me,
& her roommates
i'd never met.
so it wasnt cause i'm a racist,
you hear?
being afraid aint the same thing. lotsa
people are afraid.
lotsa people
stay with their own kind
just to be comfortable.
its not racist to be
comfortable.
it's just human nature.
it's not racist for me to go only to white places,
to be afraid to go
to the bar b que on san pablo or the
fong fong bakery on grant st.
it's just a question of
familiarity.
like those black mens bodies
were very familiar.

o i want to do it all i want
to drain my tortured mind i
want to hold yr thin body
i want to love the children all
the time, all the time

i know i'm here somewhere oops
well look over here
here, stupid, here cant you
hear me whatareyou deaf here i am
i'm sure i'm right
here
see. ah see. i have
found my breast & am
holding it with my right hand

ah. yr angry.
amazing how people hop to my side if i just lie down naked.
amazing how they attack me if i dont.
at least you dont claim to love me.
i'm always grateful for small favours.

i beat off after every meal.
havent had a cavity for years!

tk this despair in yr mouth
& drink it.

Variation on a theme by Eric Hoffer—

anybody can get into a poem but it takes
a jewish comedian to get back out.

thats the trouble with somebody
you have power over.
they're so goddamn weak
they cant exist without you.

i usedta be a 145 pound weakling.
i was a pushover for any man.
then i took karate & now i
hit men with my purse!

I BEG YR PARDON, BUT
NOBODY LIKES TO GET RAPED

we're making you our
sacrificial lamb
& you *like* it   you *like* it

                    i have learned
              to use black ink
                    to use heavy cover paper:
                    to title the edge of the book.
         i have learned to avoid handwriting, & even
         typewriters (readers can tell you are poor) i have
    learned that grants are for other people, if anybody,
    & that bookstores do not want to take me seriously. i have learned
              that only solitary women will distribute my books;
         women as solitary as i was when i wrote them, printed them
              with less than black ink. i have learned
many publishers suffer as i do: there is less money than we
would like to have; the artists are temperamental. and we do,
on occasion, get ripped off, which always hurts
                              (since we want to live as if the new world
                                   has been born)
         i have learned the slicks will not buy my poems or my stories or
              my articles; i am dependent on counterculture or no one would ever
         read me; i have learned to ask never less than $150 or they think i am
small shit & dont pay at all;
                    i have learned poetry is an occupation like most any other,
                    & i am forgetting how to write.

how can people stand to be around me? i'm always babbling
about unity, life forces, the Deep Meaning of it All.
ugh i could live in constant embarrassment.

he said, lying there, looking
at me, his voice deep in my ear,
"i love you, alta" his voice
in my whole body like a blessing.

i intend to win
the game even tho
i'm not playing.

support the war. beat yr kid.

whites in front of me,
blacks behind me,
i didnt fit anywhere.
i stood in the middle of the bus
feeling like a jew.

all those men puppy dogging
round my door. it was like
playing "go in & out the window"
& they were all jealous sillies,
as if any of them had ever known me.
the woman they possessed so hard didnt even exist.
i can't even remember their names to call them & laugh over the phone.

i wake instantly if someone touches me
comes from yrs of sleeping w/ men:
protecting myself against their
protection.

ARGUMENT WITH MY MUSE

bob in the hotel room
his one suit in the wood wardrobe
next to the iron bed. tho i felt strange,
i was at home in the circle
of his arms, touching
his round butt. i saw a butt
like his yesterday & all of a sudden
the man was naked
& i was back in the room with bob

tell how it was

warm.
our bodies so different:
his arms male, huge, brown & smooth
mine female, small, freckled white with lite brown hair

that doesnt tell it.
tell it.

people stared at us in the hofbrau. he was finally working--
janitor for the phone company. they promised to train him:

                                                    he was
optimistic.

how did it feel

good. it felt good.
he was proud & muscled, i
loved standing with him

what were yr motives?

curiosity & glee.
besides,
i was lonely.

what did you speak of

we rarely spoke.
he told me i had pretty eyes, that our arms
looked pretty side by side, that my husband was a fool
to leave me.
he played with my daughter
& stood to shake hands with my foster son, who was shocked
& said to me after "mom, you can do what you want, but
i gotta say, i dont like seein you with a coon."

what was it like

it was like thick honey the doctor told you not to eat.
i trusted him, his body,
the scent of him, the smooth skin
not like my skin, so smooth it was,
so cooly smooth

yr not telling it good:

it was good.
he felt like home to me.
my brother said, thats the kind of man who makes you glad to be there.

those sound like cliches

well, he's gone--it's hard to reconstruct--
the picture is in my mind, but like he & i rarely spoke,
the picture has no words.
there is him, naked, muscled & brown,
me white on the white sheets,
him gentle & unafraid
of me. he was not afraid
of me. that's rare in a man.

why did you speak of what others thot

i liked to show off. he was
so handsome.

tell it, it was strange to others,
they stared like when you held a woman,
tell it

you just told it.

do you think of him still?

last night, that other man,
his eyes so knowing, it was
us against all those pudgy
white men, his warm eyes, his firm butt

where is he now?

where am i now
where are you now

word games! give up,
you cant tell it!

i give up. i
cant tell it.

(all there is is this pen & gold
paper when really there was

    him
  in that barren room)

OLD SORROWS LANCING MY HEART

terri.
yr like a girl i loved
10 years ago. she was
thin, brilliant,
she walked defensive,
she said stuff everybody heard
whether they listened or not.
she called me mom
& kissed me.
when they saw we were happy,
they took her away.

i promised i would but i can't.
so what else is new?

why did you quit writing.
because of the grief.
because she was gone, & i loved her.
& the others ridiculed me.
i heard their salty laughter, tho
their faces were turned away.
& no one asked to print my poems.
i quit writing because of the
grief.

CHILD CARE CENTER

did sandra steal brenda from louise?
did connie steal sandra from brenda?
did i steal brenda from sandra?
did brenda steal me from laurel?
will susie steal brenda from me?
will matthew steal me from brenda?
tune into the women's center for
the next exciting adventures of your
local mothers at work.

living in sin

i have
my own car
my own bed
my own body

what does it mean i am yrs i am mine am i nobodys? what does it mean
i have no last name? if i do not belong to someone, how will we ever
discover who i am?

OWED TO MY WASHING MACHINE

(snap)
o yeah
(snap) (snap)
o yeah o yeah
(snap) (snap) (snap)
o yeah o yeah o yeah
(snap) (snap)
o yeah

the cotton i'm wearing was picked by slave labor.
you think i'm lying. cotton in 1972 cant be slave,
there arent any slaves.
well, i got news.
cotton is picked by prisoners.
people in prison pick cotton.
they get paid 2-1/2¢ an hour.
cops search their bodies before they march back
into their cells.
course, if you think only terrible people
go to prison, that solves the problem.

used to be only blacks were slaves.
everyone white knew they were bad.
they're not bad anymore unless they do somethin bad.
all those black prisoners pickin cotton for our underwear
musta done somethin bad.
rockefeller's committed a couple sins too, but he's too busy
to pick my cotton.
those black men in prison arent too busy, tho.
that's all they
                have
        to do.

i was gonna
write another poem but
i'd rather eat pickles & scratch.

3 dogs shittin in the park.
& people worry about
what i do in private!

who is lonelier than an unloved lesbian?
even mary yesterday
when i put my arm around her
did not touch me back.

to the movement women who want me to stop futzing around
with poetry & write plays—

anyone who tells me what to do
sounds just like anyone else
who tells me what to do.

REWRITTEN LETTER FROM A REJECTED SUITOR

if yr a Real Woman,
wheres yr hot pants?
how come you got fat thighs?
your sposed to be demure, yr sposed
to wait for men & wiggle yr ass.
yr lovers are sposed to be older, not younger,
taller, not shorter. yr sposed to want character
in a man, not stamina. (stamina
                             stamin)
if yr a Real Woman,
what the hell is yr last name?

L. A. WOMENS FESTIVAL

they called & said its no good here!
everyone is angry & the wives are
suspicious.
i knew then i had to be there.

SUBURBIA

what do you own when you own yr own cage?
theres no water supply, no vegetable garden,
no cow or chickens. if the trucks dont bring food,
or if you get fired, you can die of hunger.
we are all free   to die of hunger.
now, i'm not the first to figure that out.

& does yr bottom smell, well hell.
yr bottom oughtta smell, well hell
whose bottom doesnt smell, well hell.
& so yr bottom smells, hell.

Game Preserve—

Marriage is an attempt to pickle ourselves.

this ain't a poem, it's just something i have to say:
if yr planning an abortion, because yr afraid
of social censure, or afraid you wont be able
to support yr child, don't do it.
society is what has to give,
not our children.

if yr not good to me,
you'll have to watch your step.
i have friends in low places.

2 gay males resting on the grass
one is staring funny at my bloomin ass;
"hey, fella," i say "remember yr gay,"
"you got it wrong babe, i go either way!"

we share guilt
as if it were a quilt to keep us all
warmly interconnected.

2 lil white rabbits humping in the sno
one named shkspr, the other named mo.
"i need a job, shkspr, i need a job, mo;"
"tough shit, altie, ho ho ho!"

bleak:
riding a bouncy bus past
dannys old drinking parlors
in dirty air oakland after
applying for welfare.

41

& there was fish w/ melted cheese & almonds,
a salad neither of us liked (raisins w/ bean sprouts?)
& the paintings, & the plants, & the lamps & candles
a new light way of seeing
but there was no touching.
except when i insisted.
we might have been married 50 years.

i've had some strange relationships.
i seem to return to them like a maze i cant get out of,
like a puzzle i prefer.
rather the passive man who likes me
w/o ever insisting on my body
than the endless football players
& pornographic poets. they are tiresome
even before we begin.

so you lay there watchin tv.
i stared at you, thinking 'a city full of guys
droolin down my shirt, & this dude
wants to watch tv.' something seemed
amiss. either i was getting rejected, or
we had reached that comfortable place
where we dont have to put out
to hold affection.
is this what i wanted, or isnt it?
(we didnt even hold *hands*...)

& i leave early to return to the city full
of men who cannot keep their hands off, & i think:
i want both sides
of this coin.

PEGGY

(as i stared at her breasts,
& longed to hold a woman)

we shared lockers & her silky hair
flashing rainbows / she pulled out her books,
cheerfully complaining "how come when i like neatness,
i have to share lockers with you?" & smiling at me
thru her glasses she stood & i bent to toss in my books
& slam the locker shut, our books back to back but
she & i never touching.

& what if i had said,
"do you ever want to touch another girl?" or more openly,
"can i kiss yr breasts?
peggy?"
who would she have told,
after staring at me in shock
or turning away in disgust?
what if, that night in the back seat,
i had curved my hand over her breast, what if
she had silently turned her mouth
to me to kiss?

she called me after she got married
& i angrily hung up & havent called back. what if
i had asked & she
                    had not refused me

UNKNOWN QUANTITY

like puzzle pieces, we
desperately try to fill each other's spaces;
trying to recapture what we've lost.

hunger for me hunger hunger for me
hunger i am right here you
can touch me if you reach you
can kiss my opening lips you
can feel my waters burst hunger
for me hunger hunger for me
you will never forget me your
dreams will remind you ignore me
& your dreams will cause you to
cry out my name i will visit you
as you have visited me i will
cause you to
hunger

i watch you wave
outside the window
& wish, o i wish,
you were waving hello
instead of goodbye

"There's two kinds of loneliness:
loneliness with a man, &
loneliness without a man."

Loraine Hansberry

& when the loneliness comes
sometimes i cant stand it.
i would do anything, risk
anything, to ease the pain.
so you must not need me.
you must be able to go each day
w/o me, & each night as well.
goody goody for you.
i seek desperately yr substitute,
or wrap my arms around myself
in wonder.

the poppies still grow on the hillside
as if i were not
bone / aching for you.

if you werent afraid of me,
you'd let me know
who you are.

i been in fighting stance so long
it's hard to unfight: thighs tense
for protection i curl against yr
leather jacket that likes me,
yr bearded kisses thrillchill my throat.
for awhile i just want to lie here
feeling wanted.

your face a mask
that covered other faces
in the dark i saw you
when she was kissing my breasts
but when i told you, you didnt
even look at me,
you didnt even want me
did you.

i felt gross
i felt him looking at me
as if i were gross. i felt him
asking "what more do you want?
what more, than a man's love?" & i
was too ashamed to answer i have no
shame, i want everything, i want
everyone in the world to love me,
you'd be amazed
what i want.
wouldn't you.

i wont call i wont call i wont call

how can you go so long w/o seeing me?
is it so easy to live each day w/o what we had?
(what did we have?)

i wont call i wont call i wont call i wont call

dont you know what it's like for me
to live each day w/o yr voice /
to promise myself not to crawl back,
to promise myself to wait
if you care, you'll call
once anyway

i wont call i wont

you werent that nice, what the hell
its not like you never let me
down / who needs it

i wont call

how do you do it, w/o me?
i dont w/o you. call me,
call me, cant you
hear my mind
begging

i wont call you i wont wont wont wont

the saleswoman arched her eyebrows at me,
casting one hostile glance at my tennis shoe
with the big toenail poking out. "yes?"
she waited. "i uh i need a raincoat."
"i see." we walk to the rack & i'm sweating
wishing nylons didnt always gather around my
ankles cause maybe she'd like me more if i wore
nylons. 2 stores down i bought a big black
raincoat with a hood so i could hide like
phantom of the opera & no one could recognize
me except by the big toenail poking out the
right tennis shoe.

the girls with their young breasts
black hair hiding their necks
they are laughing at the boys
"ai muchachos!" & i hide
my feelings for them, i
look out the window of the bus
at shops with broken windows

he asked me what was i fantasizing when i beat off in his friend's
                                          bathroom
& i knew what i was supposed to say so i said "i was thinking of
                                          you, dear"
but that was a lie.
i was just looking at my pretty titties
& feelin generally good.

here come the crazies
alma & alta bitching & laughing uncontrollably.
alma singing always and hurt-
ing inside & alta lonely & hanging on tite.

printing alone nitetime in the garage
w/a moth for company
suicidally banging herself against the light

tonite i felt guilty peeling a peach.
the whole day was like that.

"you play piano beautifully"
i want to tell her
but she is a stranger.
i walk past the open door.

ever since i suggested
we make love
she hasnt let me
touch her

am i so vile

CABLE CAR / SAN FRANCISCO

i came to see the view
but all i cld see was
her young brown hair held
w/ a red rubber band.

if you came
i would be casual.
i would fix tea & watch
yr eyes & say how
are you but if
you asked "are
you glad to see me?"
my protection wld dissolve
& you wld see the tears
of need in my eyes.

Simon:
i wrote about how you hurt me
but i never wrote about how i hurt you.
you wanted to be hurt in a way
i couldn't answer but neither of us
wanted me to hurt you the way i did.
i don't understand how love goes,
how i go, watching you hurt.
cant say i'm sorry? yr sorry?
we're all sorry? drop the hankie?
pain is really funny all i can do
is laugh too loud.
i didn't want to hurt you.
i wanted to love you.
we wanted to love but the formula was wrong.
one john plus one alta does not equal a lifetime.
if we'd known that at the start, would it have made any difference?

the old wicker chair unravelling.
& him snoring, asleep on my right.
& too early we have to wake & get the children
& bring them home & any day now
i'll be happy.
i mean really. really happy.

at church camp, for the wild west costume party,
i dressed as a whore.
i drew laces on me high yellow socks (for boots),
piled my silky brown hair hi on my head,
hiked up the front of my skirt so my soft white thighs
showed. i was a knockout, but they could hardly
give me first prize. church camp. so a girl
who had covered herself, veiled herself with white
head to toe, was given first prize. she was a bride.
& i, the whore, got 2nd prize.
it was just like real life!

THE ART OF ENFORCED DEPRIVATION

i remember back in hi school
corliss & i were practicing dancing
i was the boy: my hand was round
her waist & the other hand holding her
hand. (that was how we danced back in those days)
her breast was poking me right there & i thot
"wow! boys sure get the good part!"

i looked at her face to see
if it felt as good to her as it did to me
but she wouldnt look at me.
i still dont know.

NAVY WIFE

i remember what it was like in long beach, cal.
it was lonely.
so lonely, my god, i washed dishes every morning just to have
something to do.
one woman had to leave her 3 toddlers home alone to go to work
sometimes i
looked out for them, sometimes i didnt. i brought plants & rocks
to the apartment
to make it less ugly. the window looked out on an empty lot &
a bar where
i saw 2 men fight one day. blood on their hands & faces. the con
gregational church
let me play their attic piano in the mornings. once a woman came
up while i was
into Rachmaninoff & said would i quit there was a luncheon
downstairs. on the way
out i saw them refuse to give a hungry man some lime jello.
i bought a 25¢
chocolate cream pie & went back to the ratty old empty apartment
& cried for awhile
& then ate the whole pie, had a lot of good times in long beach, cal.

daily courage doesnt count
we dont get diplomas for it.
i worked hard for 5 years with one man,
then had 3 years graduate training with another.
but people called me a divorcee, & acted as if
i had done something wrong.
no one was happy for me,
no one gave me a coming out party.
but i tell you, i came out of those marriages
one smart bitch.

I: 1963

i remember scraping my thighs
because they were ugly, ugly.
i remember hating my thighs
because my husband would sooner
spill his seed on empty sheets
than lie between my legs.
once i screamed at him
"how can you waste it when
you know i need it?"
& i'd scream at the mirror
& scratch my cheeks
because they were ugly, ugly.

II: 1971

yesterday i danced in white levis.
i felt the power:
long heavy legs bloom into
full hips; full,
strong shoulders, slimming down
to my waist to burst into
full muscular hips
               & thighs:
when i wear my boots
no one dares insult me.

daddy, you
are the Man in my Life.
if i cant have you, i wont
have anybody. you held me
at night, cradled me, you
gave me toddies when i couldnt sleep.
you were the first man
to beat me. we used to walk
to the park, & you'd lie in the grass
while i slid from the very top
of the slide to the bottom.
you would count in spanish
as you pushed me in the swing. &
together, swinging in the hammock,
you'd make up lil orly stories for me
& bill art.
now the learned doctors
say you are dying. & tho
i have cursed god for malpractice, i've seen
you go from standing to sitting to lying.
the learned doctors & god
cant seem to fix you.
if my daddy were here now,
he'd kno what to do.

why do the men resent me so?
tell me i'm ugly?
i'm not ugly.
maybe they're off their nuts.

PRODIGAL

for Mom

"She's just had too much pain" jack explained her to me.
there is such a thing as too much pain.
& i avoided her soft warm belly, turned my cheek for her to kiss,
always feeling taller, stronger,
a body apart.
not connected, as to my own daughters.
but she knew when i tried suicide & called before i died.
she had to be quiet enough somewhere in her, to hear my cries,
she had to have saved a special place or we would have fallen apart:
even his death could not have restored us if we had not saved that place.
those years we barely spoke were real,
but she never laughed at me
& she never called me names.

IN EGYPT, CANARIES WERE BLINDED
BECAUSE THEN THEY SANG SWEETER

my brother sings like a canary.
not sings, thats not
it.
i mean he's funny, he's
so funny, jokes
one after the other, quick
jokes & we all are
laughing.
we forget pain, we listen
laughing at his jokes
the kitchen light is always on:
my brother sings so sweet:
can you hear him laughing like a
mutilated canary.

my father was a strong man last april.
now he cannot roll over unless we pull on him.
i have to wash the shit off when no one else is there.
what good is toilet training when yr 63 & full of cancer.

i am afraid to say the children are husky: we are all
so fragile. one bad day, one disease & we've had it
maybe.
superimposed on my father's frail arm i see the children
reaching up, brown & chubby. i am 30 years older than them.
he is 30 years older than me. what is my road, then.

he used to feel better when i was there.
i used to go to make him feel better, & so
we could talk, last time i went he said
"i thot you came to fix me! well, you didnt fix me!
get out! get out & let me die!"

so i did.
he said that thursday. i went back friday.
he said it friday too. i havent gone back.

a woman who calls her self liberated or is called liberated by a man
(she's a happy darkie, not one of them bad niggers) & then says she doesnt
go for all that women's lib nonsense is doing what i call the
PRESENTATION SHUFFLE

heres my ass
kiss it   kiss it
i'm just a happy lil chickie
massa massa
no hard feelings
no feelings
no hard
(impotence is golden)

i wont castrate you,
you cant even get it up.

that chick is SO REVOLUTIONARY
she dresses poor on purpose.
she eschews the boozhwa comforts like
washing machines, male lovers, &
flush toilets. i mean she is
EVERY KIND of revolutionary!
she'd bum off her friends before she'd work
in a counter-revolutionary government job!
(how come she can afford to be so revolutionary?)
i mean, this chick is SO REVOLUTIONARY,
she laughs at housewives, agrees that
we're an inferior breed.
she would never have a kid if she could have
an abortion instead. get it? this chick is
SELF FULFILLED!
super chick   ta daa!
even her period glows in the dark.

SAN LORENZO: BAKERY

& how could i convey my deep affection?
the women resting their elbows on the counter,
their coats tugging over full hips;
if i drew their picture who would know
i love them. & the blue flowers on the table
would be called plastic, because they are
plastic. the people would be called plastic, too,
but i tell you they are not.
that girl is eager in her new purple dress.
that woman cries when her son doesnt write.
& her tears are as real as those of any revolutionary.
& when the old woman smiles "doing yr lessons" i want
her to approve me. i want you
to approve her. i want us all to
love each other.

II

i want to tell how i love them.
the heavy thighed woman buying donuts,
the horny teenagers poking out their plumed breasts,
the decorated, watchful saleswomen.
i want to tell how
when they frown at me
it hurts me for i want their love.
i dont want to be so unwanted,
they are different from me yet i love them.
that slim grey haird woman in the big car looks like my aunt dora.

STORY

"she & i each got married.
it was the only job we could find.
but we talked our husbands into sharing
the same house. we were together
every day. you know, men think nothing
of it when they see women hugging."

"we used to wonder if they got comfort
from each other; discussing their
frigid wives."

"they decided they'd be artists, & spent
their time shut in a room, smearing colours,
while our heads would be flashing the reds
of love."

the indian boy was ugly
except when he looked at me.
then i would hold my breath
at his beauty.

you dont know she's deaf until she moves her hands to speak
& her laughter is so lovely you wish she could hear it too

I.

sitting at the candlelit table
is the beautiful lady who
uses her beauty like a key,
the price of admission,
&,once there, she
stands tall,
as if no one could
buy her at all.

she is constantly
in love, constantly
falling in love
she uses love like spice
& she can never get enough
          if every hour
were the approach of a different lover,
she would feel neglected
in the space they took to change places.

she uses her beauty like a key.
& she turns men with her little key.
today there were 4 who wanted to be her lover.
she stares at the candle & wonders why
the women didnt stay with her. wonders why
the beauty key only works with men
& why only the men come back for more.

she is the same person, is she not,
the same thigh touches the thighs of all those
who sit next to her.
she pushes the candle's wax drops in circles
on the table & prays that all those men
will add up to
one lover.

II.

why am i
never content
broken lemon rind
on the white porcelain circle.
& the flowered bowl,
the vase,
the flame brighter than the marigolds.

charlie i could
write power/poems
of you to say to
women in road
side cafes/ no
salt i could
write you &
me poems of not
now fucking poems
of let go
of me let go poems
of me wanting more
of you of them
wanting more of you
of them wanting
more of me let
go/help i need
space charlie not
enuf charlie
to go around/ not
enuf altie to pass
around/ pass.
go. let go power
poems of stunt
-ed desire/ stunt, man
repeat after me. go
-od bye. (charlie)

"my love be yr gentlest keeper"—Paul Mariah.

solitary for 2 years.
who committed the sin that locked you there?
4 lonely boys, lonely & untouched,
& you touched them
but you touched them where
o where paul
& who committed the sin?

for a waiter at the pot luck restaurant—

tell how these, the men who serve,
are the true men, the ones who can still
touch themselves w joy.
how the dead men they serve are
dead, their hearts pumping a simile
for blood, their flaccid impotent bodies
waiting in chairs for the men who can still walk
to serve them.

i push you away. you
are not my daddy. you have
those balls, & that thing, but
yr not him & besides all
that stuff is dirty i
certainly wouldnt touch daddy
so lookit
i wont touch you.

he's 45, but he's been goodlooking
all his life, & he aint gonna
stop now. he struts to the
counter in his levi jacket &
jeans that slip a little
down his flat butt / the
back pockets greasy
from when he wipes his
hands at work. he
checks out the waitress,
puffs out his chest
orders black coffee
& i half expect him
to stir it with his thumb.

PEACOCK

"gotta be a good butt somewheres here"
poking with a thick nailed third finger
in the purple ash tray.
"goddamn Jews smoke all the way down"
pulling away paper near the filter,
catching tobacco flakes in his palm.
"I ever tell you about the war?
the army?"
"which war?"
"*which* war?? yeah, sweetheart, & i
was in the salvation army."

building, yr too ugly
for anyone to live in.
but someome lives in you.
looks out dirty windows
to busses on the street.
listens to the sound of people walking.
the only way to hear a bird in this
ugly part of oakland wld be to
trap it in a cage & make it sing.
like what happens to poets.
& the fat boy tugs his sweater
on down past his belly
as if he were
ashamed of his own flesh.

IN THE GIRLS BATHROOM AT FREMONT HI

cigarette butts sogging in the sink
smoke so thick it hurts to breathe
this is what it's like if we arent watched, they say:
this filling up of space

as i wash my hands, a lovely
hello from a girl with red hair.
then she nudges another 'she's a teacher!'
& i have been identified
as one who fits in spaces.

you hide yr face when
you think yr not pretty
you turn yr head
away from me so i wont see
so i lose myself in yr
hair, yr hands, i'll take
whatever you can give.

A CONFUSION OF MUSK

when we knelt side by side
the smell of us rose between our legs
& i couldnt tell, after the first shock
(that means i want her!)
i couldnt tell if it were yrs or mine.

BABY BLUES

i'm too young to be a grownup.
mom & i fight; now i've got this baby
are we gonna fight like me & mom?
my body's wearing down, bleeding,
milk draining from me /
how can i feed her joyfully with contaminated milk?

shit i'm scared.
there's the kid & i'm not sposed to fuck up
or it'll grow up queer & then everyone will know
i'm a lousy mother

it's crying. i'm sposed to know why.
"why is yr baby crying?" i'm sposed to
tell it apart in a roomful of crying babies.
"that yr baby crying?" "no, mine doesnt sound like that."
"o, you mothers are so amazing!"
mother. mother is a swear word.
ma bell. motherfucker. mutha.
now i'm one. whaddam i babbling
about? i've been one for 5 years.
how can i be scared all over again?
"o its just baby blues, dear."
yeh? how come women get depressed
3 days after the birth? doesnt anyone think
thats a good question? "women just do. you know
how women are." no, motherfucker, how are we?
maybe we got legitimate fears. anybody ever think of that.
maybe babies remind us of the draft in 18 years. ddt in our milk,
the way fathers ignore their kids. who's gonna love us so we can
love the baby when it cries, who's gonna say "i'll change her now, love."
maybe we got reasons to cry.

but even if we didnt, can you hear me,
even if we didnt, our tears deserve
a little respect.

i got those pretty woman blues wondrin what do they see.
i got those pretty woman blues wondrin why their eyes fasten on me.
they call me foxy & say will you be mine?
they show me to the boys at work, they put me in a line.
my legs compare, my face does too, & after that, what do i do
but wonder if those legs were gone would i have someone to count on.
i got those pretty woman blues.
other women stay away, they act afraid of me.
they never want me round to meet the men they see.
unless i bring a man along to prove i'm off the market,
no woman wants her lover to look my way.

i got those pretty, pretty woman blues.

julia unlocked me with her key.
she said "only the wounded can calm a wound."
so i ripped off the covering & am letting it air.
see how sore.

there is in my cunt
yr body. that small inflamed
part of yr body made specially
to go there. yr face indistinct in
moonlight you were all those
men & only you, you were the
one who passed the tests, you
got to put yr body in mine & the others
didnt
any more.

THROUGH

thru is spelled thu roo
ugh. everythings alrite.
the war is off in nam,
or oakland, or some
place you dont live.
thru is spelled thu
roo ugh.
have a drink,or a
drag, or a pill, or a
cigarette, or eat cake.
thru is spelled
thu roo ugh
we will get to the
other side other
side other
side
other
w/o feeling the war
the things we have
to take the poison we
have to swallow is
prescribed
its ok thru
is spelled
thu roo ugh

RED SHIRT

there had been that intimacy between us.
i stood behind him; his body
had not lain in my arms for
2 years. but our child was climbing
into the truck. there had been
that intimacy between us.

when they see us,
our hands folded in our laps,
how many understand the pressure
of one hand against the other;
the controlled rage
& the love.

i sit reading bad poems
wondering where are yr poems
you used to hand me like leaves
you found on the way to my house
& my husband watching

if that leaf on my desk
had been brought by you
wld i feel
a little less sad

i comfort the baby from her dream.
"why you were talking to them."
"i wasnt, bunnies, i was asleep in my bed.
that was probly a dream."
"that was a dream?"
"i guess so."
"why we were in it?"

it was in the mind of the great mystery that all peoples should learn
to live together. the land can no longer belong to any one people.
                              —american indian songbook

i see a land where different peoples grow
together & sex stirs them up the colors
mixing the women co
habiting with men the children born
of these mixtures not having one parent
or the other the mixture complete
& i see frantic thoroughbreds
destroying the different others
in an attempt to stop the vision & i see
the children walking away from them,
learning to love the others, & now learning
to love themselves. even the white men
touching their own bodies with love, & without
shame. i see the sex becoming love i see
women loving women loving men loving men loving
women loving children loving animals loving plants
the earth rejoicing in grass & corn & the never innocent
children taking only what they need, with reverence &
i see the end of self hate
projected as war.

someone doesnt want us to know.
you are the sun glowing inside my body.
someone doesnt want us to know
we are the circling planets.
if we realize our existence, who can destroy our power?
if we realize our power, who can control us?
that's why they put imitation bodies on billboards:
glory like our suns cannot be controlled, the whole world
a glorious galaxy of lovers.
no one would tear up flowers anymore & maybe
we would taste freedom in our hungry souls
like we taste loves liquids in our hungry mouths

i was lying on my back & turned to look at you.
your face right there & i dared you
to make it real but we just looked &
the blood rushing in my ears i
couldnt hear a word you spoke
until you looked away

touch her navel. there.
the belly so soft & smooth.
she's ready to trust you
touch her / wet / she's ready
wet & ready & her mouth
sighing yr name.

my heart is in my womb.
i feel it beating there, that's where
it beats from.
the stupid men called her a whore.
i feel my heartbeat in my womb.

kissing him
was all the wonder & colours
                    of the rainbow.
kissing him, remember it,
was all the wonder.
& colours of the rainbow.

i touch myself
in an effort to approximate
what you could do. just imagining
you here i smile with delight.

i slept alone last nite but when you know you dont have to,
its kind of an adventure. to just dream yr own dreams
& not wake up feeling
guilty

i love everyone who
lays their arms on the table
& rests their head on their arms.

just as i was beginning to worry
you might be bored down there eating
me for so long, you sighed,
"um, you taste so good!"

i would write a love story. one to warm my shoulders in this cold room. one of strong brown arms, fine fingers, that happily touch me all over my body. of lips that had to learn to kiss, of nights we lie next to one another, curled, of looking at each other when we are desperate to see one another.

i would write of such a love, such a body, such a person that loves me so. i would write, & be glad, & forget that i sit alone in this room, with no one to come see me.

remember instead the ringing telephone, the soft low voice, the promise of naked warmth. i want my breasts against his chest. i want his hands on my hips, moving smoothly down the curve of my hips as i breathe in his smell. i am tired of people finding each other ugly. i want to sing the beauty of all bodies, of the joy of touch, the warmth & softness of heavy bodies, the tight energy of hard bodies, the soft, melting breasts of mothers; the small buds of breasts of girls. the soft curled cocks of men before they want me; the way they fill & rise to fill me up with their love. the curve of the butt below the balls as he lies on his back, smiling at me, his cock moist & hot. his smooth brown chest, belly flat below his risen cock. the beauty of my soft white breasts coming down on him, my full thighs around his tiny hips. the textures, the colors, the hard places & the soft places, the strength of our bodies as we come together

his tongue licking my breast as he rubs me; my finger touching inside his precious circle--the precious circle that guards his cock but pulls back for me, pulls back when he enters me, so that we are both fully exposed, & vulnerable to each others love.

80